Honorée Corder
Author, *Vision to Reality & Business Dating*

Revised, Expanded & Updated

Tall Order!
Organize Your Life and Double Your Success in Half the Time

10th Anniversary Edition

Published by Honorée Enterprises Publishing, LLC.

Copyright 2015 ©Honorée Enterprises Publishing, LLC & Honorée Corder

ISBN: 978-0-9961861-3-1

Discover other titles by Honorée Corder at
http://www.honoreecorder.com.

Additional titles by Honorée Corder

Prosperity for Writers: A Writer's Guide to Creating Abundance

Prosperity for Writers Productivity Journal: A Writer's Workbook to Creating Abundance

Business Dating: Applying Relationship Rules in Business for Ultimate Success

Vision to Reality: How Short Term Massive Action Equals Long Term Maximum Results

If Divorce is a Game, These are the Rules: 8 Rules for Thriving Before, During and After Divorce

Tall Order! 7 Master Strategies to Organize Your Life and Double Your Success in Half the Time

The Successful Single Mom

The Successful Single Mom Cooks! Cookbook

The Successful Single Mom Gets Rich!

The Successful Single Mom Finds Love

The Successful Single Mom Gets Fit!

Madre Soltera y Exitosa

Play to Pay: How to Market Your College-Bound Student-Athlete for Scholarship Money

Paying for College: How to Save 25-50% on Your Child's College Education

The Successful Single Dad

Get Even More

AS A THANK YOU FOR reading this book, I want to give you two free chapters of:

Business Dating: Applying Relationship Rules in Business for Ultimate Success

This is my networking book that shows you exactly how the rules of personal dating apply to your professional relationships. Go here and tell me where to send your free chapters:

http://honoreecorder.com/businessdating

Table of Contents

A Note from the Author

I can't believe it's been 10 years.

When I wrote the original version of this book at Mark Victor Hansen's urging (you'll know him as the co-author of the best-selling *Chicken Soup for the Soul* book series), I had no idea how it would impact my future.

What I thought would be my one and only book became the first of what has become more than a dozen books over the past decade. Becoming an author has opened so many doors for me, and I am eternally grateful for everyone and everything that has happened as a result of first writing this book.

If you have ever read the original version of this book, thank you! In this revised, updated, and expanded version, I have discovered what has happened to the people whose stories I included in the first version. The best part was discovering how much I have learned in the past ten years! While I knew the original *Tall Order!* provided value to its readers, I know this all-grown-up version contains within it a depth of knowledge and information that will help readers—you—on an entirely different level.

I hope you love it.

To your best success!

Honorée Corder
Visionary, Strategist, Writer, Coach, Mom

Introduction

Dear Reader,

Where are you in your life and career right now? Maybe a better question is, *Where are you right now in relation to where you ultimately want to be?*

Do you desire to make more money in less time? (Who doesn't?) Create the business and career of your dreams? (Wouldn't that be amazing?) Enjoy a greater level of success while maintaining balance and fulfillment in every area of your life? (Of course you do!) If your answer to any or all of the above questions is a resounding *yes!* then this book is for you!

Ten years ago, I wrote this book to share several of the most powerful strategies I found myself consistently using and sharing with my coaching and corporate clients. Here I am, a decade later, finding they still apply as much, if not more so, than they did back then. This book includes seven of the most effective strategies for business and life success. Although you'll find I've made distinctions, discovered important nuances, and improved upon some of my original ideas, those original ideas still apply. What I've discovered is that these strategies have stood the test of time.

If you want to take your life and business to the next level, you need to gain clarity. Clarity includes an inspiring vision, precise goals, and a focused and exciting plan. Without clarity, you might move quickly yet not necessarily in the direction you want to go.

If you want to achieve that vision and those goals more quickly and easily, you'll need to glean information from successful individuals who have gone there before you. Otherwise, you may reach your destination, but it'll take a lot longer than you'd like it to.

You need to have strategic success systems in place to allow you to be more effective and more efficient. Success doesn't come because you've discovered a secret, it arrives once you've identified and implemented the right systems.

You'll need to be cognizant of whom and what you allow to surround you. Having the right inner circle and advisors can, and will, make all the difference. You'll need to have someone in your life who holds your vision for you and with you and who cheers you on and gives you permission to go for it.

Finally, you have got to have a coach, but not just any coach: the right coach! Your coach will help you strategize the biggest vision possible for you, flesh out the right plan, identify goals to get you where you want to go, provide support and ideas right when you need them, and hold you accountable when the going gets tough.

Tall Order! is the book to get you going in the right direction, your right direction. Are you ready? Let's go! To your best success!

Honorée Corder

Visionary, Strategist, Writer, Coach, Mom

Some men see things as they are and say, "Why?"—I dream of things that never were and say, "Why not?"
—George Bernard Shaw

I see people as better than they see themselves, hold that vision with and for them, and help them live into that vision until it becomes their reality.
–Honorée Corder

TALL ORDER!

Have What You Want Your Way

When you go to a restaurant, you have the opportunity to "have it your way." If what you ordered isn't right the first time, you can send it back as many times as necessary until it's done right. After all, you've gone to the trouble of getting yourself to the table, of course you expect your order to be exactly the way you want it, right? Right.

The same is true with your business and your life. This is your life, and you *can* have it the way you want it!

I have some great news for you: every single moment of your life is a moment of creation. With this book, you are entering your next moments of creation with the assistance you need to help you order (if you will) your destiny exactly the way you want it.

I present to you a collection of strategies, formulas, tips, tools, and ideas that I use and have used for the better part of fifteen years. I know they work because they work for me and my clients every single day.

Here's what I suggest you do: read the entire book all the way through. Then start again at the beginning, taking each strategy and think about it as you go. Decide if it resonates for you. If it does, put it into action.

Take notes about it, work with it, tweak and refine it as necessary until you've "cracked your code," i.e., discovered how to make it work for you. The fantastic thing about each strategy is that it's like an ingredient for your favorite cookie. You can add the ingredients to your strategic recipe until it fits you perfectly.

Soon you'll be experiencing a greater level of success and fulfillment than you ever thought was possible. Keep going until you've achieved the success you desire.

We go where our vision is.
—Joseph Murphy

*Travel in the direction of your clear vision ...
and take your road map just in case.*
—Honorée Corder (2005)

*Turn your vision to reality by defining what
you want, and surrounding yourself with
everything you need to make it happen.*
—Honorée Corder (2015)

Master Strategy #1: Create Your Vision

When my daughter was five, her karate instructor repeated over and over: *"Focus on the target!"* Presently, she's a sophomore in high school and is continually asked, *"What are you going to do after you graduate from high school?"*

While the jury is still out, this I know for sure: she's amazing, and whatever she does, she's going to do *very well*. I know this because when she sets her mind to something, she creates a clear picture in her mind and then does whatever she has to do to make it happen. I see in her a focus and tenacity I only wish I had developed much earlier in my life.

Every year, at least one school activity requires a fundraiser. This year, to raise money for her dance class, she got to sell pies. While other kids in her class sold one or two, Lexi got on the phone and called every relative possible (and my wonderful husband comes from a large Southern family, which certainly is helpful), went to all of our neighbors, and even had me call a few friends and clients she knew loved her and would say yes to just about anything she asked. Dozens of pies later, her *entire class* got a movie and pizza day because she had sold so many pies. She wanted to sell the most pies, and she did. Vision accomplished.

How does this apply to you? Well, I have just one question: *do you have a precise, defined, and clear vision?* If you do, you are firmly placed among the top 1 percent of people on this planet. But if you aren't there yet, don't be too hard on yourself. I advise you not to wait another day without taking the time to create one.

What Is a Vision?

Vision is what you see in your mind's eye, not necessarily something you're able to see externally. It's the mental picture you have when you think of a desired outcome.

Would you go on a trip without knowing your destination? Of course not. You think of where you'd like to go (somewhere warm, maybe with a beach?), then you think about places you've been (Puerto Vallarta? Hawaii? Harbour Island?), and the next thing you know, you're picturing yourself sipping on an umbrella drink, sitting in a beach chair, and enjoying a beautiful sunset.

Hold on, I have to book a quick trip.

Okay, I'm back. I got so excited about my vision I couldn't wait to *make it happen*. The same sense of urgency can occur within you.

Think for just a moment about what your life and business or career could be like. I don't mean if it was a little better than it is right now. Nope, no way, I mean if it was flippin' amazing! You wake up every day and have to pinch yourself because everything is just so good.

Now, hold that thought for a few minutes and keep reading.

Master Strategy #1 is the process of envisioning and creating your vision. Personally, this is my favorite strategy, and I'm sure you can guess why. But if not, I'll tell you: it gives me something to get and stay excited about. My visions fuel me to keep moving forward. I know you, too, will find it to be a most exciting strategy and big fun to create.

At first, the process and outcomes of visioning may seem vague and intangible. Perhaps you find it hard, or have found it difficult in the past, to picture what you want clearly. But I promise you, the long-term benefits of taking the time to get clear about your future sooner rather than later are beneficial and substantial, and the results can be simply amazing. Let me explain.

Visioning breaks you out of boundary thinking. As you open your mind and your mind's eye to new possibilities, you will begin to shed previous limitations. As you picture yourself doubling your income, starting a business that supports you, growing your career to expert status, or even taking twice as many vacations next year as you did the prior three years, you are expanding your mind and your consciousness. A new idea of what is possible literally, and permanently, changes your mind. Your horizon has moved, and you now have new places in which to play.

One's mind, once stretched by a new idea, never regains its original dimensions.
–Oliver Wendell Holmes, Sr.

Visioning provides continuity and avoids the stutter effect of planning fits

and starts. Having a defined, clear vision that you review often, and I do recommend reviewing it often (at least twice daily), will help you avoid "New Year's Eve Syndrome." Sometimes visions are crafted, only to be forgotten in about two weeks (until the next New Year)! Once you've put in the effort to create your vision, you'll want to see it through to fruition, right?

Your vision automatically identifies your future direction and purpose. Your vision grabs hold of your imagination, keeps you interested, strengthens your commitment, and promotes laser-like focus. When you hold a clear picture in your mind of where you're going, it is always present, ready to pull you in the right direction. Wouldn't it be fun for your vision to be working on your behalf, helping you along? Trust me, when you've done the work to make it crystal clear, it is!

Visioning encourages openness to unique and creative solutions. As you hold your clearly defined vision, the ways to make that vision happen become clear. Your subconscious mind silently and steadily works for you to spot potential opportunities, prospects, potential partners, and possibilities you might otherwise miss. You'll start to notice things you might have missed without that clear mental picture.

Visioning promotes and builds confidence. Have you ever noticed how someone with purpose and vision carries themselves in a certain way? They are positive, upbeat, and yes, confident. Your confidence will become magnetic, attracting your clearly defined vision to you. As an added plus, you'll be attracting other awesomeness as well.

Don't all of the above benefits of visioning sound amazing? I bet you're ready to start crafting your vision. There's just one more important thing to note:

Coach's Insight: You have created in your life what you have previously held as a vision, even if you didn't realize that's what you were doing. If your current circumstances aren't quite to your liking, it is entirely possible you envisioned them into existence. *But before you get upset (you know who you are), remember this:* what you visualize comes to pass.

Now is the time to use your subconscious mind with a picturing tool

to create what you truly desire, this time on purpose.

Think of vision as clear imagination, only now it's directed imagination: by you, for you, about you. You are creating your future, one magical moment at a time.

Your Visioning Exercise

Start by daydreaming. Begin to imagine what your business and life would look like if time, energy, people, space, and money were no object. If you start to think, *that's too big or too much for me*, suspend disbelief and take the lid off of those perceived limitations.

What areas of your business need a clearer vision? Jot those down.

How can your marketing, advertising, customer acquisition, or customer service efforts be markedly improved? Define what they look like at their best and most profitable.

What areas of your life aren't working as well as you would like? Identify them then write three to five sentences (or paragraphs) as you want to see them.

Are you in an empowering relationship that is mutually beneficial? Do you want to be?

What would an amazing, inspiring relationship look like?

Are you as strong, fit, financially sound, balanced, and fulfilled as you wish to be? Even if you are, there's always another level.

This is a bit of an oversimplification, but to begin to craft your vision, you'll create an overarching, perhaps longer-tem vision (such as over the period of a year or five years), then break it down into shorter terms (like 100 days—I'll talk about that in a future chapter).

Next, you'll break your bigger vision down into areas of focus, such as work/career, personal relationships, physical, and even mental goals. Then you'll create a unique vision for each of those areas. As I suggested, begin by starting five to ten years in the future. Describe in vivid detail what your ideal day looks like. Include a description of your surroundings (office, employees, clients, family, and friends). Now work backward from that vision. Describe what that vision looks like in six months, then three, and finally next week. Ask yourself, *What is my preferred future?* being sure to

- Draw on your beliefs, mission, and mental picture of your model environment.
- Describe in detail what you want to see in the future.
- Be specific to each area of your life.
- Be positive and inspired.
- Be open to massive changes!

Here are some questions to help you start creating your vision:

- In your vision, what time does your day start? End?
- Who is with you? Your success is determined in large part by the people you surround yourself with, and it is time to become clear about who you want to attract into your life in the future. We'll address this more in Chapter 6.
- What activities are included in your ideal day (exercise, meetings, phone calls, fun, meditation)?
- What types of customers do you have? Create an ideal client list with at least 25 characteristics of your model client. Include everything from age,

income, and attitude to how they receive information and services from you and how often they refer new business to you.

- Where is your office located? Do you have multiple locations? Do you work from home, in an office, or in both places? Be sure to include the type of equipment you work with, all those neat furnishings, plants, pictures, etc.
- Do you have employees? How many?
- What is your ideal living space? Where is it located? What do you drive?
- Where do you vacation? With whom? How often?
- Define your friends and other significant relationships.

Brainstorm. Be specific. Be playful. Be creative. Have fun painting a mental picture of your perfect life. Make it the way you want it, after all, it's your life!

Coach's Note: In case you are tempted to do this exercise only in your head, I know from experience it is important to put your vision in writing. There is power in the written word. Just the act of writing down what you want sets the creative process in motion. You'll have plenty of time to visualize later, but after you first think it, you must ink it.

Vision Killers

As you engage in the visioning process, you might find there are people or circumstances that aren't quite as excited about what you're attempting to achieve as you are. You'll want to be alert to the following vision killers:

- Tradition. Be careful of the phrase, "But we've always done it this way." You'll make the biggest impact on your future by thinking differently than you have in the past.

- Ridicule. Most often the people who criticize are those who have neglected to create their own vision and who come from a place of fear instead of power. You may represent the vision they are afraid to attempt to achieve. Do I really need to say you should tune them out? Okay, tune them out. You're going to listen to only the people who cheer you on (right?).

- Stereotypes of people, conditions, roles, and outcomes. You can have what you want, regardless of what other people are thinking, saying, or doing.

- Nay-sayers. In an effort to be incredibly redundant, I say this: refuse to listen to anyone who doesn't absolutely 100 percent support your vision. Period.

Remember: there is no right or wrong way to write a vision! You should describe in full detail exactly what you desire. It may take you 20 pages or more, or it may be as simple as one page using bullet points. When you're done, you'll know it.

I love crafting visions for myself, my life, my family, and each of my businesses. I get very excited over and over again as I read my vision, which ultimately is what I know I'm creating, each morning and evening.

Coach's Tip: I use Evernote to house my vision documents and have the app on my phone, iPad, and computer. That way, I can access and review, my vision during my morning practices and any other time the mood strikes me.

Coach's Challenge: Right now is a terrific time to stop and create your vision. Before you can create any goal (and goals are up next), a clear picture of your overall vision must be present in your mind's eye. Do it now, or schedule a nonnegotiable appointment with yourself to do this initial, most important step as soon as possible. You are creating your legacy, starting with your vision.

Your legacy is the powerful, positive impact you have on others.
—Honorée Corder

A great example of someone who has created a compelling vision is Margaret Trost, Founder of the What If? Foundation. After a visit to Haiti in 2000, Margaret was inspired, asked the question, "What if I could help?" and created a vision for feeding the hungry children she met in the Ti Plas Kazo neighborhood of Port-au-Prince. It started out as a dream then grew into a vision to provide the resources for 500 meals per week, even though she wasn't sure exactly how to do it.

Margaret's vision was linked with the vision of the Ti Plas Kazo community to bring desperately needed food and educational opportunities to their children, and so they created a partnership. Step by step, they put their vision into action, and a community-based food program was born. It started out serving 500 meals each week to hungry children and expanded from there.

Today, Margaret's vision and leadership has made it possible for the What If? Foundation to provide funding for 5,000 meals a week, 150 school scholarships a year, an after-school program for 240 youth, and a summer camp for 650 children. In addition, construction of a new neighborhood school has just been completed. "My vision for what's possible has grown as I've grown on the inside as a person, as a leader."

Margaret believes and knows from experience that a vision must come from within, a product of the heart. When it's right, it resonates on a deep level and gives a feeling of "Yes! ... I'm inspired, excited, connected with my soul. I have chills... I'm not sure how I'm going to manifest this, but I am determined to take the steps to do what I can to make it happen!"

She also shared that the true power of vision comes into play as the daily challenges of life surface and as setbacks appear. A true, from-the-heart vision will keep you focused and moving forward, even when it might be easier to quit or give up. She lives by the wonderful Creole saying, "Piti piti na rive," which translates to "Little by little, we will arrive."

Learn more about the What If? Foundation by visiting http://www.whatiffoundation.org.

You are not here merely to make a living. You are here to enable the world to live more amply, with greater vision, and with a finer spirit of hope and achievement. You are here to enrich the world. You impoverish yourself if you forget this errand.
—Woodrow Wilson

All successful people have a goal. No one can get anywhere unless he knows where he wants to go and what he wants to be or do.
—Norman Vincent Peale

If you are not able to see your goals, they will take longer to achieve, and sometimes "longer" is "never."
—Honorée Corder

Master Strategy #2:
Visible Goals

Now that your vision is in your mind's eye, you might be thinking a combination of *Wow, let's go!* and *Uh-oh, what do I do next?* Maybe even a little, *Oh dear, what if it really happens?*

The great news is that by having a clear, compelling vision, you have a wonderful place to begin your journey.

How are you feeling?

Are you all fired up and ready to go? A great vision can inspire, motivate, and drive you forward, almost effortlessly.

While you might feel excited, you also might feel a little apprehensive. It is entirely normal to have a gut check moment, one in which you feel like you just might have decided to bite off more than you can chew. Who does that? Well, you do! I get how you're feeling, and my advice for you is simple: just go with it.

Master Strategy #2 is the wonderful process of setting visible goals. I know our goals should be big enough to make us feel stretched because it is only when we go beyond our perceived limits that our own personal magic can happen. Underneath any limiting beliefs or thoughts you may hold, you know in your heart that you can accomplish them. But doing so requires you to dig deeper than you've ever done before. You can accomplish so much more than you might believe you can right now, of that I am convinced because I have seen it so many times before.

Achieving a great goal takes extraordinary effort, intention, laser focus, and maybe even a bit of luck. Yet, it can't be so big that your mind checks out because you don't even have a sliver of belief you can make them happen. In fact, I believe a goal properly set makes you feel just a little bit nauseated. You're becoming your highest and best self, which takes an incredible amount of courage. Sometimes that courage has a few uncomfortable side effects, and one of them (at least for me) is *nausea*. Yup, if you're feeling nauseated, you've probably got the right goal.

Set the Goals to Get the Goals

You identified areas of focus important to you when crafting your vision. Based on those areas, your next step is to identify categories within those areas, such as: employees, money, exercise, family and personal time, personal development, and other things you want to acquire, do, accomplish, or achieve.

Sometimes finding the right answers or goals, or obtaining clarity, requires that you ask the right questions.

Here are just a few questions to prime your mind and get you started:

Business and Career Goals

How much new business will you produce?

How many new customers will you obtain?

How many new employees will you hire?

How much money will you generate?

What new or continuing education will you need?

Personal Goals

Where will you live? If you haven't thought about it yet, do it now. Who lives with you?

Where will you go on vacation? When? How often? Who is going with you?

What new car will you drive?

How close are you to your physical prime? How much do you weigh, or what is your body fat percentage, or how strong are you, or how much more flexible are you?

With each successive question, you'll achieve greater clarity. As you gain clarity, you'll be able to set an incredible goal for each area.

Perhaps you have a huge or long-term vision. You'll want to set an interim goal, so take that bigger goal and break it down into something a little easier to chew on. If you have 100 pounds to lose, the long-term goal is just that: to lose 100 pounds Your 30-day goal might be to lose 12 pounds, or 3 pounds per week. I don't know about you, but losing 12 pounds seems a zillion times easier than 100 pounds! But once you've lost 12 pounds, you then have only 88 to go. Repeat that seven more times, and you've lost 96 pounds. You can achieve this goal, one month and 12 pounds at a time.

Suppose you want to make $30,000 this month, and each sale of your product or service is $2,500. Do the math. You'll need twelve customers to reach your goal. You might even go so far as to figure out how many people you'll likely have to prospect in order to make one sale.

For example, if you have to talk to five people to sell one $2,500 product, to sell to twelve people, you need to talk to sixty. Sixty conversations, appointments, or pitches will yield you 12 new pieces of business and get you your $30,000 goal.

Goal #1: $30,000 income

Goal #2: Sell twelve $2,500 products.

Goal #3: Set 60 appointments.

Bam. You have your marching orders and know exactly what you need to do to achieve the goal.

Coach's Note: When crafting your goals, you'll want and need to be as specific as possible. Make sure that *anyone* would know whether you have achieved your goal. "Goal #1:

$30,000 income" is different (and also much better) than "Goal #1: I make more money than last month."

Words like "more," "a lot," and "some" are too vague. There is power for you in precision, and there is power in the words you choose. Choosing carefully and wisely will do wonders for you, and be incredibly instrumental in whether you achieve your goals.

Commandments for Goal Setting

1. Write down your goals. This is perhaps the most important aspect of goal setting. Writing down your goals creates the road map to your success.

If I had a nickel from every person who has told me, "I have my goals right here in my head," I could buy everyone who reads this book a first-class round-trip ticket from Austin to London. I mean, we could all travel together on an amazing trip. Having your goals only in your head is about as effective as going to the gym *only in your mind*. (I know, I wish that worked, too.)

2. Review your goals twice a day. Although the simple act of writing down your goals can set the process of achieving them in motion, I cannot stress enough how important it is to review them frequently. I review my goals twice daily: once during my morning ritual and again during my evening ritual. Combined with other powerful success practices, I am never more than half a day away from reviewing and remembering what is most important to me. I recommend you do the same. Reviewing your goals once or twice daily is so crucial to your success, you must make it part of your routine.

Think of it this way: left to chance, you might remember to review your goals every once in awhile, thereby decreasing the chance, *any chance,* you'll achieve them to a tiny fraction of what is possible, for you *and* for them! When you put in place a twice-daily practice to review your goals, and by virtue of that practice remind yourself every single day exactly what you want to achieve in your life, you dramatically increase your likelihood of success. So, you'll notice I'm suggesting only that you review them. You can do that in a few minutes, it won't deplete your energy (if anything, it'll get you excited and top off your energy), and it doesn't cost anything.

Yes, that's right my friend, I've just given you a way to achieve your goals and greater levels of success for free, in under ten minutes a day. You're welcome.

But wait, there's so much more!

As I've said, the more focused you are on your goals, the more likely you are to accomplish them. Each morning when you wake up, read your list of goals. Spend a few moments visualizing each goal as completed. See your new completely furnished home, smell the leather seats in your hot new sports car, feel the cold, hard cash in your hands, imagine yourself on the airplane taking a selfie as you fly off with your family. Visualize yourself already on that vacation to gorgeous Mexico, the sun warm on your skin as you sip piña coladas beside the clear, blue ocean. Vividly picturing your goals completed triggers your brain to automatically move you toward your vision as quickly as possible.

Each night just before bed, repeat the process. This will keep both your conscious and subconscious mind working towards your goals.

Follow this twice-a-day goal-review process every day, and you'll be on your way to achieve unlimited success in every aspect of your life.

Write it down. Written goals have a way of transforming wishes into wants, can'ts into cans, dreams into plans, and plans into reality. Don't just think it—ink it!
—Author Unknown

If you don't see it, you will be never be it.
—Author Known (me)

3. State your goals in the positive.

Forward-facing, positive, and inspirational: three great words that can and should describe your goals. When you write them down, be sure they are in forward-facing, positive, and inspirational language.

Base your goals solely on your future vision. In other words, of course you'll want to work toward what you want in the future, not what you want to leave behind. You can use language to your distinct advantage. The right language serves to focus your brain in the exact direction you want it to take you. Part of the reason for writing down, examining, and re-examining your goals is to create a set of instructions for your subconscious mind to carry out. Your subconscious mind is a very efficient, powerful tool that does not distinguish the real from the imagined. It does not judge; your subconscious mind's only function is to carry out instructions. The more positive the instructions you give it, the more positive results you will get and the faster you will get them.

Coach's Thought: Positive thinking should not be limited to goal setting, either. Apply it in everyday life to help you grow as a human being, too.

4. Make your goals congruent with each other.

In other words, one goal must not contradict any of your other goals. All of your goals must be in alignment with one another, and in every way possible, work in concert with your other goals.

Coach's Example: A goal to buy a $750,000 home is incongruent with an income goal of $50,000 per year. This is an example of non-integrated thinking and will sabotage all of the hard work you put into your goals. Non-integrated thinking can also hamper your everyday thoughts as well.

Once you have created a complete draft of your goals, make sure they are symbiotic with one another. A goal of working one day a week is incongruent with launching a billion dollar startup, whereas a goal of making $100,000 in a year is congruent with saving 10%, or $10,000. I'm sure you get the idea: taking a quick review of all of your goals together can reveal discrepancies and allow you to make adjustments from the start.

5. Make your goals specific, precise, and clearly defined.

Just like your vision, writing your goals in complete, vivid detail will be instrumental in achieving them. Boring goals yield boring results. Technicolor goals yield Technicolor results. Instead of writing "a new home," describe the home you desire: "A 7,500 square foot contemporary with five bedrooms, three baths, an office with a separate entrance, a view of the mountains on the water, and 20 acres of land."

Giving your subconscious mind a clear picture is the same as giving it a detailed set of instructions. Clear, specific information given to the subconscious mind yields the desired final outcome. In addition, those clear instructions help your subconscious mind to work efficiently and quickly to turn your vision and goals into your real-life, real-time reality.

Remember, your subconscious mind—much like a toddler's—doesn't understand the word no. Have you ever noticed little kids running alongside a pool while their parents shout "No running!"? It's not very effective, is it? If instead the adults called out "Walk!" the child more readily understands what she should do and will change her behavior more rapidly in response. It's a far more effective directive. Similarly, if you're focusing your subconscious mind on something like "no more debt," all it hears is "more debt." Frame your expectations positively and your subconscious mind will be able to deliver them faster.

Can you close your eyes and visualize the home I described above? Walk around the house. Stand in the sitting area off of the master bedroom and see the fog lifting off the snow-capped mountains. Look down at the garden full of tomatoes, green beans, and cucumbers. Off to the right is another garden, this one full of different varieties of roses. Can you see it? So can your subconscious mind! Craft your own vision and goals just as clearly, and you'll be able to see them in your mind's eye. Your subconscious mind will work relentlessly to bring your vision to reality as quickly as possible, in the precise way you have imagined.

Coach's Note: Your subconscious mind has always worked "for you" in the way I described above. Yet perhaps because you didn't know how to harness and direct it, it has seemed to work against you in the past. It has created what you have previously held in your mind as your vision and will continue to do so. Now that you know how to work it, *work it!* Hey, it's free to do, takes a negligible amount of time, and will get you everything you want because with a clear vision, you are now ready to make different choices, diligently work toward your goals, and recognize opportunities. There's just no argument against doing it!

6. Include a timeline.

Timelines are vital to goal achievement. By when, exactly, must each of your goals be achieved? "This year," "soon," "in a little while," or "later" won't cut it. Pick a date. If a target date is not on your calendar, it's not going to happen. Your timeline will need to be written like this: "By June 30th, I have 12 new customers who have purchased my services at $2,500 each." You must be able to measure exactly where you stand now against where you want to be in the future.

> *A goal is a dream with a deadline.*
> —Napoleon Hill

> *To live your dreams, turn them into goals with rock-solid deadlines.*
> —Honorée Corder

7. Make sure your goals are BIG enough!

I'm sure you've heard Norman Vincent Peale's quote, "Shoot for the moon. Even if you miss, you'll land among the stars."

Goals can, and should, inspire you to move forward, perhaps with a little bit of a knot in your stomach. If your goals are too easy, you won't be as motivated to achieve them. If they're too hard, you might become overwhelmed and not even take the first, necessary steps.

The best and most exciting part about the perfectly set goal is the fact that we have the opportunity to become an entirely new person in the pursuit of that goal, even if we don't achieve it.

When a goal is big enough for you, you must dig deep within yourself to find the wells of determination and heart previously undiscovered. In case you don't know, you have more potential than you realize and can do far more than you might think at the present moment. I've seen, time and time again, people discover their own greatness with only a smidge of encouragement. Consider this your smidge! You owe it to yourself to set goals big enough to help you create an environment in which you can become all you are meant to be.

Coach's Challenge: Set your goals now.

Is there ever going to be a better time? I honestly don't think so. The worst thing, in my mind, would be for you to read this book and then do nothing with it. I know good intentions (and where they lead) as well as anyone, and it would be tragic if you missed any or every opportunity that could come your way as a result of making the time to set the goals that can truly change the course of your life.

Taking action right away reinforces to your subconscious mind that you are serious about creating your vision and achieving your goals.

If you cannot take the time right now to work through these steps and set awe-inspiring goals for yourself, I understand. You probably didn't expect a couple of hours of homework when you started this chapter. But I'm not letting you off the hook entirely! Pull out your calendar and identify a two-hour block of time within the next three days. You are important, your future goals are important, and both deserve a spot for your time and undivided attention as soon as possible.

All good? Keep reading ...

8. You can always change or adjust your goals.

Sometimes *life happens.* In the pursuit of our visions and goals, we realize we have to revise a goal as circumstances and other goals change.

As it turns out, about 20 percent of the time, my clients will reach a 100-day goal (more on that in the next chapter) within the first two weeks of our work together. When this amazingness happens, we take a hard look at adjusting the goal "up," coming at the desired vision or goal in an entirely different way, or changing the goal to something else entirely.

Another 2 percent of the time, a goal will be missed by a little ... or a lot ... in the allotted time. I have some thoughts on this (shocking, I know), whether the goal was hit very early, is in process but has not yet been hit, or has been missed entirely.

1. **The goal needed a little more time.** When you set the goal, you didn't have all of the necessary information. It could be you didn't realize how undeveloped the goal really was, how much time it would need to truly ripen. Many of my clients have a lot of low-hanging fruit and a bit of effort on their part yields quick results. The opposite is also true. Sometimes, many times, things take longer than we'd like, the people we're working with need longer to make a decision or take action, or unexpected circumstances cause a delay.

I once hit a goal on the 100th day at 2 p.m., after spending 100 days at 0 percent to goal, despite a promising start and *lots* of potential business in my pipeline. Taking massive action and being intentional in just about every moment is sometimes not enough. I've seen many clients hit goals within a week or two after their 100 days ended.

2. **The wrong goal was set.** The goal you went after might not have been the right goal for you after all. Once you got into the process of moving toward it, you realized (sooner or later) it wasn't quite what you wanted to achieve. You might have learned something on the way, had an external experience that determined your desired outcome, or at some point you realized all of the signs pointed you in a different direction.

The minute you discover you're working toward the wrong goal, set another goal. Use the information you have and identify a new target. There's no sense making great time climbing a ladder that's set up against the wrong wall. If you need to change a goal, don't consider it a failure. Instead, consider it a victory because you had the insight to realize the goal you set wasn't perfect and you had the courage to make a change!

3. **Life happens to screw up the goal.** Sometimes an unavoidable roadblock pops up which completely alters your goal, or even your overall plan. Even as I was writing this book, a client of mine was fired immediately following

Session four of eight total 100-day sessions, which was his day 43. We had just gotten him into the momentum stage and identified his ideal client and prospective strategic partners with whom he should pursue developing relationships. Fortunately, he landed a new job within two weeks, but we had to put our heads together and figure out how to maximize the rest of his 100 days.

Do the best you can with what you have— know that all you can do, is all you can expect to do.

What to Keep in Mind

I recommend that you keep your goals to yourself. Share them only with those people you absolutely, 100 percent know will support and encourage you. Stay away from dream stealers. Negative attitudes from friends and family can drag you down at the speed of sound. It's critical that your self-talk (the thoughts in your head) and the talk around you are positive.

Coach's Suggestion: Make copies of your goals to put in different places in your office, car, and home. This will help to keep you on track. I post my goals everywhere: above my treadmill, on my bathroom mirror, on my desk, on the visor in my cars. They are on 3x5 cards, and I also use glass markers to write on mirrors, glass, and tile surfaces. I want to be reminded of what I want to have, do, be, and create in every possible moment. What you may not know is that even if you don't consciously see your posted goals, your subconscious mind doesn't miss a thing, including these subtle reminders. And the best part is that your subconscious mind is working on your behalf to make your vision a reality. Every time your subconscious mind sees those goals, whether you notice them consciously or not, it digests reinforcement and keeps working for you. Kinda cool, right?

Keahi Pelayo, a realtor in Honolulu, inspired me recently when I asked him to share his insights about goal setting with me. As a highly successful person, he had achieved all of his material goals ... the house, the cars, the vacations, the trinkets.

What then, I wondered, does one use to keep oneself motivated to continue to move forward, when you have more than enough? The answer, my friends, is leverage. Leverage is the act of using external factors to keep you on track; it improves and enhances your power to act effectively.

Keahi shared a powerful goal-setting experience with me. The housing market in Honolulu was exceptionally strong, and he had set the goal of doing more business in that month than ever before. I was intrigued. His goal was to do seven listings and eight sales that month. Further, he was using the power of leverage to reach his goal. I was more intrigued.

His son, then age six, had told his dad he really wanted to have a new train. Keahi told his son about his big goals and made a deal with him: if Keahi achieved his goals, his son would get his train. If he didn't, there would be no train. His son was to check with him often (and, as any parent knows, in child-speak, that is about every 10 minutes) to see how dad was coming on the goals, if he had achieved them, and when the train would be forthcoming.

Needless to say, his son was relentless (leverage can be very powerful!). All of Keahi's goals were achieved with this additional external desire to please his son, and his son got his train.

The most important lesson Keahi learned was, not achieving more wealth, or even in attaining more things, it was to please his son. When he shifted from a focus on tangibles to non-tangibles, he realized how much more rewarding it was to focus on the non-tangibles.

I personally know the benefit of releasing an attachment from things to people and experiences. You might find once you've achieved all of the material success you desire, a shift to how you feel, and how you can help others feel, might become more a more dominant focus or intention for your goals.

Coach's Practice in Action: Using affirmations will rapidly increase your results! I also call affirmations *vision-to-reality statements*. Your goals stated in the present tense as positive statements, produce fast, often amazing results. Be sure to include words that excite and motivate you in your affirmations!

Affirmations are vital ingredients in the recipe for success and personal well-being. After all, whether you think you can or can't, you're right. Many of the world's most successful people have testified to the power of affirmations. Affirmations reflect what you believe to be true.

Here are some examples of affirmations:

I can't do it.
I hate myself.
I'm ugly.
I'm stupid.
I knew I would mess up.

Wait, what?! Surprised you, didn't I? You thought affirmations were only positive things you say to yourself. Affirmations are simply thoughts you repeat or "affirm" so often you believe they're true. They can be positive or negative. They solidify any thought or idea you have. They can work to your advantage or disadvantage. They will be your strongest supporters or your greatest obstacles. The beauty of affirmations is that you control them once you're aware that you're already using them.

Coach's Hint: You can change what you believe to be true by using affirmations. You are already using affirmations, but you might not be using them with intention and purpose. Now that you know, or I've reminded you of something you already knew, you can take the time to create new ones that move you in the direction of your vision and goals.

You might be wondering where to start with affirmations. I suggest you start listening to your internal dialog. You may be surprised to find out how often you say negative things to yourself about you, your relationships, career, and even your potential.

Suspending judgment, pull out your journal and record your negative self-talk for just one day. Write down when you notice yourself making statements like those on the previous page. You'll know it's not a positive statement when something you say out loud, or to yourself, doesn't make you feel amazing—quite the opposite in fact. The results will shock you—and not in a good way! You will most likely be surprised at how many negative thoughts you have and how often you say something negative to yourself about you!

I know I do not feel good when I catch myself thinking, "Man, that was dumb," or (insert sarcastic tone here) "Way to go, Honorée!" I do not feel empowered. And I certainly don't feel like rising up and being more of who I can be. My best self isn't around in those moments, and I sure could use her. I know you could use your best self more often, too, and just noticing how often you're scaring your best self off is a great place to start.

Once you have identified the negative affirmations, replace them with positive, confident, and empowering thoughts. You have a couple of great opportunities with those negative comments. You can

1. Flip 'em around. "I can't do it," becomes, "With the right intention and determination, I abso-frickin-lutely can do it!"

2. Spin 'em. "I knew I would mess up," becomes, "Well that was fun! Now I know what not to do next time!"

Remember nothing we experience comes labeled; we label it. The power to choose is yours.

Let's take a look at the difference in those first affirmations when I flip 'em and spin 'em:

- I can do it! In fact, I can do anything!
- I love myself more and more every day!
- I am beautiful inside and out!
- I am smart!
- I am successful!

- I know I can do it!

If you plant rose seeds you get roses. Plant seeds of happiness, success, hope, and love; they will come back to you in abundance. This is the law of nature. Choose to surround yourself with positive influences. Affirm positive statements daily until they become second nature. You'll soon begin to harvest a crop of positive results in your life.

Negatives belong in a photographer's studio, not in your mind.

Here is an example of pairing a goal with an affirmation:

Goal: I will increase my business by 50 monthly consumers by March 31, 2006.

Affirmation: "I am jazzed as my business now increases by 50 consumers each month."

My personal favorite affirmation: "I am an irresistible magnet for unlimited money, clients, goods, and services every single day!"

While you're working on your goals, schedule in some additional time and write an affirmation for each one. Say your affirmations out loud, every single day (twice a day—I dare ya)! I encourage you never to underestimate the power of what you say to yourself on purpose. Affirmations are more powerful than you know (unless you're an avid practitioner, then you *do* know).

Remember this: they work best when you say them with passion, energy, and enthusiasm. I do mine while exercising, in the shower, driving, or waiting in line at the grocery store (these could be silent for you; they are for me). You'll be amazed by the results, I promise.

For my top 10 favorite affirmations, log onto my website at http://www.HonoreeCorder.com/Resources to download your free copy! (Password: **success**)

TALL ORDER!

Action is the foundational key to all success.
—Anthony Robbins

Action without an action plan is wasted action.
—Honorée Corder (2005)

You'd better have a rock-solid action plan.
—Honorée Corder (2015)

Master Strategy #3:
The 100-Day Rule

What I'm doing right now in my business will show up as results in about three months. Why? Because of lag time. Although we live in an instant coffee, microwaveable world, the results of our efforts, sadly, are not instantaneous. In fact, true momentum, *solid* momentum, is gained over time. I have discovered that momentum and the results from the actions one takes to get that momentum, take about 100 days to become evident. I call this the 100-Day Rule, and you'll need to create a 100-Day Plan to benefit from it. A well-designed 100-Day Plan will serve to keep you focused and moving in the right direction.

I recently attended a seminar where the 100-Day Rule was discussed. It got me reflecting on my network marketing days and how much of an impact this rule made on my business then. I also realized the impact it has on my current businesses! One hundred days ago I was neck-deep in three huge professional projects, and today I am basking in the sunlight of my efforts. At the same time, I took a break from the intensity and focus of my health and fitness goals ... and I am decidedly *not* basking in the sunlight of those results.

Master Strategy #3 is the 100-Day Rule, and here's how it works: whatever you are doing right now, today, will affect your life and business in 100 days. If you're busy searching for new business two hours a day, you'll have fantastic results in 100 days. If you occupy yourself with paperwork and minutiae, allowing them to consume all of your time, then 100 days from now you're going to be frustrated because you won't be generating the results I know you truly desire. Like me, if you eat cupcakes a few times a week because your neighbor has a cupcake business (ahem), while at the same time working insane hours and skipping more than two or three workouts a week, at some point your favorite pants might not fit. I'm just sayin' ...

After a short time working together, clients will often ask me, "What is the problem? Why aren't things happening for me now? I've been at this for two weeks already!" My response is (always), "What were you doing 100 days ago?" Those are the results you're getting today. It could benefit you to think back and recognize where you may or may not have been acting in your best interest. When you open your eyes and realize the importance that today's activities and thoughts have on your future, you will have a higher likelihood of putting tremendous forethought into pre-planning them. Make sense?

I often see my clients focus, take massive action, network, make phone calls, have a calendar full of meetings, and see no immediate results in month one. They see some measurable results in month two, and then, bang! Amazing results and true momentum occur for them in months three, four, and beyond.

Keeping the 100-day Rule in mind will keep you going because you will remember and understand what is happening, or not happening quite yet, and why. You're less likely to become discouraged and quit when you understand this concept.

Let's have some fun looking at the days ahead, while taking the pressure off as you work your current plan. I suggest you not beat yourself up for what you did, or didn't do, 100 days ago. It's what you do today that is important. When you accept this rule, it's much easier to persevere in the face of downturns because you know all you have to do is create a new plan and work that plan.

We have time enough if we will but use it aright.
—Johann Wolfgang von Goethe

Determine how you will use your time well in advance ... and the results will speak for themselves.
—Honorée Corder (2005)

Before you do anything, determine what would be the most purposeful and intentional action you could take based upon your vision.
—Honorée Corder (2015)

Coach's Command: To create a strong, stable, constantly growing business, always be thinking and working 100 days out.

Whether you work for someone else or you're an entrepreneur making your way in the world, you want the business you're in to pay off, and you want to be healthy, feeling great, and surrounded by amazing people (personally and professionally) while you're at it. Or is that just me? (I didn't think so.)

Coach's Note: I thoroughly explain my Short Term Massive Action (STMA) 100-Day Plan and Program in my book *Vision to Reality*, which you may want to read at some point. This section provides a 30,000-foot overview.

Let's start with designing your very first 100-Day Plan.

Begin your 100-Day Plan with a mini-vision statement, accompanied by a purpose statement. These two statements will be your guiding light, reminding you not only what you're excited about, but why.

Next, create empowering descriptors for yourself, such as "progressive, educated leader" or "marketing maven." In other words, do you want to be "in shape" or a "goddess?" Give yourself a reputation to live up to, using the most energizing, positive words you can think of. Words are incredibly powerful, be particularly alert to the words you use to describe yourself and the actions you want to take. These powerful descriptions of you will help create and maintain a desire to continue, even when the going gets tough.

Your plan should include three areas of focus. Depending on which areas of your business need growth, development, and management, pick the three most important.

Coach's Insight: The brain can handle only three ideas at one time. Have you heard of 1-2-3-many? This phrase refers to how much information the brain can hold. When providing directions to your home, most people can remember "take a left at the Texaco, then a right on Elm; it's the third house on the right." Those three pieces of information can be recalled easily. More than that is too much.

The same principle of three applies to your business.

Do you need more contacts? Are you getting, but not closing, presentations? Do you have plenty of customers, but want to improve your relationship with them? Pick the top three, most crucial areas to focus on for this particular 100-Day Plan. Keep in mind that you'll be re-tooling, modifying, and updating your plan monthly. You want your plan, and your business, to be balanced.

Coach's Example: As you focus on current sales, remember to look for new business and constantly network to keep your momentum going.

Next, define your resources. I'm not talking about cash resources here. I'm talking about people you know, books, seminars, and other business tools. Your resources are invaluable; in that they are a well you can draw from to maximize results. The more resources you have available, the easier your path to success will be.

Of course, you'll add in your goals, and you'll adjust to make them fit within the 100-day timeframe.

The last part of your 100-Day Plan is the "Next Steps" section. This includes everything you can think of that needs to be done for you to reach your goals in the next 100 days. Like a to-do list, you are going to prioritize each item according to what is most important, and then what's next most important … repeating until the list is complete.

Here is an actual 100-Day Plan Example, created by Zac Sestina, a successful realtor with Keller-Williams in San Diego, which you can use as a model for your own:

100-Day Vision: Create an ever-increasing income of more than $25,000 monthly. Connect homes to new homeowners.

100-Day Purpose: Increase to 10 monthly transactions and provide increased income stability for myself and my family.

Empowering Descriptors:

- Progressive, learning-based leader
- Focused and productive
- Leads by example
- Results- and growth-driven

100-Day Intention: Increase monthly income to more than $25,000, and monthly transactions to more than 10. This will become automatic going forward.

Three areas of focus:

1. Determine marketing methods in order to activate law of attraction.

2. Create strategic partnerships and alliances.

3. Recruit listing agents for continued business expansion.

Resources:

1. Mentor
2. Networking
3. My coach

Goals:

1. Five Listings/month by end of March
2. Five Sales/month by end of March
3. Hire a listing agent by end of January

Next Steps:

1. Implement marketing-based, prospecting-enhanced lead generation system to target market.
2. Interview 10 buyer's agents to hire (must have experience working with builders to add value to existing relationships).
3. Spend one-half of current lead generation time interviewing potential staff members.
4. Create and maintain a one-year business and marketing budget. Hold myself accountable to tangible results!

5. Spend three hours per workday soliciting referrals for new business and new staff members. Remember the thank you notes!

For a blank 100-Day Plan, log onto my website at HonoreeCorder.com/Resources to download your free copy! (Password: ***success***)

Keep These Thoughts in Mind

Your plan doesn't have to be perfect, just do it! You'll be able to change, update, and refine it as often as you need to, and you have the opportunity at the end of each 100 days to do a review of what went right and create a new plan for the next 100 days.

Notice the results you're getting. If you're getting good results, keep moving. If you're not getting results, ask yourself if you've been doing the right actions for long enough or whether you need to make an adjustment or a change.

Get excited at the completion of your first 100-Day Plan because you're now well on your way to creating exactly what you want!

Coach's Insight: Upon completing each of my 100 days, I do a review, then I create another 100-Day Plan to begin within two weeks of my 100th day. I create and execute three 100-Day Plans each year ... starting with January 1st to about April 10th, then the beginning of May (the dates of this one will be May 1st to about August 10th), I take a break until after Labor Day, and my final 100 days of the year runs from the beginning of September to mid-December. This keeps me consistently moving in the right direction, with ongoing, effective check-ins to keep me on track.

Mentor: someone whose foresight can become your hindsight.
—Unknown

If you can find out what the most successful people did in any area and then you did the same thing over and over, you'd eventually get the same results they do.
—Brian Tracy

Crack your success code by duplicating, shifting, and mastering the strategies of successful people."
—Honorée Corder (2005)

Persistence and consistency are the keys to your success. Slow and steady steals the show!
—Honorée Corder (2015)

Master Strategy #4:
Find a Masterful Mentor

I see so many people trying to advance their careers and figure things out on their own. Trying to become successful on your own will take much longer for you to get to your desired destination, increase your stress, and ultimately means you might never get where you want to go. Why would you try to reinvent the wheel when there's a solution that's so simple and easy it will blow your mind?

That solution? A mentor.

Master Strategy #4 is for you to find a masterful mentor: someone who has created some, if not all, of the results you want in your life and business. Imagine that someone is willing to spend time with you to help you strategize ways to achieve your vision and goals, while helping you turn decades into days (ok, maybe weeks) by giving you key information to make your journey easier *and* save you time, energy, and money. This mentorship could be one of the biggest blessings your career can receive!

When you think of a mentor, you may visualize an experienced businessperson who will take you under their wing and teach you all about business, customers, and relationships. You wouldn't think about making a major decision without consulting her, and that is exactly right.

An ideal mentor is someone who has started a business in your industry, been successful both personally and professionally, and who has probably made many of the mistakes you hope to avoid.

I've had the privilege of having dozens of mentors throughout my various careers. When I was an executive assistant at the *National Hockey League* in my early 20s, a woman who had been in my position for more than thirty years taught me the ins and outs of working for high-powered executives. Then I started my network marketing career, and I had four different successful teams in my upline, as well as someone I've already profiled in this book, Margaret Trost, who guided me on my path to success. Finally, you'll shortly read about

Mollie Pratt, whose mentorship provided me with incredible direction.

Your mentors don't have to be people with whom you have monthly conversations over lunch. In a perfect world, you would have your mentor on speed dial and consult with them on major decisions. Ultimately, mentors can also be found in the form of seminars, group programs, and in my case audiocassette tapes. As this book is being published, I read books and listen to audiobooks and podcasts to get mentoring and coaching (which is discussed in Chapter 7), as well as attend mastermind groups and events a few times a year.

I count Jim Rohn, Zig Ziglar, and Tony Robbins among my mentors, although I've met only one of them (Tony) on a few occasions and he certainly doesn't know he was my mentor. But I have listened to every single one of his programs dozens of times over the past twenty-five years and attended his life transforming Unleash the Power Within, Life Mastery, and Date with Destiny seminars multiple times. I would definitely consider him an integral person in my life and a contributor to my success. (Thanks, Tony!)

Finding Your Perfect Mentor

If I've convinced you of the value of a mentor—and I hope I have—the first challenge you'll need to hurdle is deciding who would make the best mentor for you.

Coach's Question: Ask yourself, who has already created the life and business or career that I want? The successful person who has spent a decade or more in your chosen field is the perfect person to model your business after. Research a few people before you make a decision on whom you would like to work with the most. In an age where cyber stalking is an option (and I mean that in the most respectful and legal way possible), you can read about them online, including checking out their LinkedIn profile, reading their website, listening to or reading their interviews, and even sending them a friend request on Facebook.

Before you pick up the phone, remember that proper preparation on your end is key. Any mentor worth working with is a mentor who is most likely busy beyond words. You don't want to waste your time and certainly not that of your potential mentor. Knowing specifically how they can help you is key to a successful mentor-mentee relationship.

Coaching-in-Action: Before you can obtain the time of your future mentor, you have to make the case for why they should meet with you the first time. Start by creating a list of questions you want to ask your potential mentor. If you're lucky enough to get subsequent meetings or have several conversations, you will be able to ask lots and lots of questions. For now, identify the most important, key questions, the answers to which will have the biggest impact on you. Those are the ones you'll want to ask.

Sample questions for your mentor:

1. If you were starting all over again, what would you do differently?
2. Where do you feel the industry is going?
3. What, in your mind, is the difference between someone who is hugely successful, moderately successful, and not at all successful in our business?
4. What did you (and do you) have to believe about yourself to create the results you've created?

Getting the First Meeting & Making the Ask

Upon completing your research and preparing your questions, you'll want to make a short list of potential mentor candidates if you haven't done so already. Have more than one potential mentor in mind because you might find that your most desired mentor is already mentoring someone and might not have the time to take you on as well.

Call or email each of them and ask them to lunch or coffee. Yes, you're going to pick up the tab. Or at least you'll try. I would never let someone much younger than me, or who was asking to be my mentee, pick up the bill. *However*, I would expect them to make the attempt (or ask if they could). The attempt to pay is a sign of respect.

Tell them why you've called the meeting with them specifically. Give them high praise for their accomplishments and share why you're impressed with them. They will appreciate the fact you've taken the time to research them and their accomplishments.

Then, talk a little bit about what you're trying to accomplish. Your best bet is to prepare a few sentences about your professional and personal aspirations and be ready to share them when asked.

Finally, ask them to be your mentor, even if it's just for the duration of the present conversation. Perhaps the person you're meeting with will agree to be your mentor. That's terrific! If they are willing to offer ongoing support, you might agree to meet monthly or quarterly.

They might be available on an ongoing basis, and if so, you can agree to meet monthly or quarterly. When you are able to convince an experienced person to provide you with mentoring, that, my friends, is a complete and total win. Time is more expensive than anything else in the world, and when someone commits to giving you their time and knowledge, you've scored a massive win. (Way to go!)

But perhaps this meeting is your one and only opportunity to get some key questions answered. Whether you have only this meeting or multiple meetings over the foreseeable future, you'll want to arrive fully prepared. Bring your carefully crafted questions along. Your questions must be designed to get them talking about key insights they've made on their journey, as well as anything you'd like their input on.

Even if this meeting is the only one you ever get, you'll be able to gather some important and potentially life-changing information in a short time. I had what you might call a passing conversation with a very successful business coach when I first started my coaching business, and the value bombs she dropped have remained priceless to me over the past fifteen years. The amount of time you spend with someone may not determine the quality and value of the time you spend with them. I don't want you to miss out on any opportunities, which is why I encourage you to put as much forethought into preparing your questions as you do in choosing your mentor.

My Mentor Story

When I was ready to accelerate the growth of my network marketing business, I thought about who had the level of success, income, and lifestyle I aspired to create. A woman I had met on one occasion (and whose tapes and other materials I had used over and over) came to mind. Mollie Pratt had been in my business for over 30 years and was a true example of who I wanted to model my business after.

Because she wasn't in my upline (and therefore did not financially benefit from helping me), I approached her through a third party. Turns out, this was unnecessary because she was more than thrilled to help me.

Since we were geographically undesirable to one another (she lived in Florida, I lived in Hawaii) she happily jumped on the phone with me once or twice a month to answer my questions, provide guidance and insight, and even shared some strategy.

I had compiled a list of 12 questions that I felt would help me to set my future course and direction correctly. I was honored and thrilled when Mollie agreed to chat with me, and our initial conversations, and those that followed proved to be incredibly beneficial to me.

The Mentor Advantage

I know I achieved more over the next couple of years in my business because of our six or so months of conversations. She influenced my life and my business in such a positive way. I know having the right mentor will do the same for you. By answering your questions, helping you to think through and even avoid problems, and even adding a touch of foresight to your life and business can, and will, be immeasurably helpful.

Coach's Note: Most people are happy to give you an hour or two of their time, particularly if they know you are going to take action on the knowledge, insights, and wisdom they share with you. The most successful people also tend to be the most gracious and willing to help.

My mentor jumped at the chance to help me. She later told me that the reason she was so willing to help was because she saw my approaching her as a sign of my commitment and enthusiasm. She even said she felt my energy and excitement, which in turn helped to keep her motivated and moving forward in *her* business!

Few people can or will resist this approach: "I've admired what you've accomplished in this field. Would you allow me to take you to lunch and ask you a few questions?" When you do get that meeting, remember the more specific your questions, the more value you'll receive.

A mentor relationship can also develop into something deep, personal, and long term. A mentor is someone who serves as an example, an advisor, a sounding board, and in most cases a friend.

That last attribute is very important. A mentor cannot be effective if they don't truly care for you, and vice versa. Great mentors do what they do for one reason: they want to help you succeed. They aren't working with you to make money, to boost their egos, or to be able to claim volunteer time on their resume. They work with you because they're interested in helping people.

While this won't always be the case, know that your attitude, passion, and dedication will bear heavily on someone else's willingness to help you. Recently, someone commented to me that they had stopped helping people because the advice they shared seemed to fall on deaf ears. Your responsibility to your mentor isn't financial; it takes another form. You will be responsible for taking their advice and suggestions and putting it into action. I can attest there is nothing more frustrating than offering free advice and watching someone not take it.

As the recipient of mentoring and advice, I recommend you receive, reflect, and act on the advice if it's right for you; but you shouldn't ignore advice or dismiss it without considering the value it can bring to your life.

One last thought. You can, and probably will, have more than one mentor. You could have a mentor help you with the launch of your business or career. You could also have a relationship mentor, someone who has been happily married for four decades and is willing to share nuggets of wisdom. Mentors can be specialists in a certain aspect of your career at any given time or generalists who have done all you want to do. Talking to folks of different ages, levels of experience, and backgrounds can give you a well-rounded view of life, your industry, coming trends, and even what could happen in the future.

Reinvent the wheel? No way! The road to success has been paved by your mentors ... combine their strategies with your enthusiasm and focus, and your success is guaranteed!
—Honorée Corder (2005)

The right mentors can save you time, money, energy, and effort. At the same time, they will give you time and make you more

money than you can possibly imagine. Pretty
cool, right? I think so!
—Honorée Corder (2015)

Maximize Your Mentorship

Here are some things to think about as you seek your perfect mentor, and how to make the most of your time with them.

Earn their respect. Do what you say you're going to do, every single time, no matter what (and no excuses).

Ask nicely. And smile.

Be prepared. Always show up ready to work and to learn. Do your homework, and once you've gotten some great advice that resonates with you, use it!

Always be on time. If you're less than 10 minutes early for any meeting, you're late! I could write a lot about the virtues of being on time, but I'll share some suggestions for how to do it instead. First, allow yourself plenty of time to get where you're going. If you are meeting by phone, by all means add in some buffer time on either side of the meeting. Second, schedule an appointment with yourself ahead of time to prepare. Finally, if the worst-case scenario happens and you can't make the call or meeting on time (or at all), get in touch as soon as humanly possible, apologize profusely, and request to reschedule. Life happens, apologies go a long way, and there isn't a person on this planet who hasn't missed a meeting (myself included), so you will probably receive some grace for your mistake or situation.

Find common ground. People like others who are most like them, and your mentor won't be any different. Did you attend the same college or university? Are you from the same state or town? Perhaps you have something besides your industry in common, such as a hobby or religion. Discover your points of connection.

Respect their time. Always, always, always be respectful of your mentor's time. Respecting someone's time requires not only being early, but also keeping an eye on the clock so you know when the meeting should end. I set a timer on my phone so I get a five-minute warning. The warning helps to catalyze a wrap-up and, if needed, provide the space to set up the next meeting.

Keep their information confidential. Unless you're told differently, assume each and every piece of information and advice is a secret and must not be shared, under any circumstances, with anyone. Having been on both sides, I know my mentors have shared with me confidential or private information, and I've treated it as such. Conversely, I've shared private information I really wanted to be kept private (which I asked for and got).

Show your gratitude. Be sure to acknowledge them with a handwritten thank you note after each meeting and phone conversation. Yes, you could send an email, but that's what everyone does. You're different, special, and fantastic, and you send a handwritten note. Right?

Take notes. Remember, your mentor is giving you their time, and that is an incredibly generous thing to do. Notice everything they do right and make note of it because hopefully, someday, you will also be a mentor, too. You'll probably want to reference those notes in the immediate and distant future.

A Few Words of Caution

Sadly, we live in a world where people sometimes misrepresent themselves. Some are insecure; others are more nefarious.

Regardless, the results are the same: you may sometimes think someone is a perfect mentor for you based on what they *say* they've accomplished rather than what they have *actually* accomplished.

At the beginning of this chapter, I encouraged you to do some research on your mentor-candidates. Doing some due diligence wouldn't be a bad idea, either. While in the legal profession you can easily confirm that someone graduated from law school, what firms they've worked for, and what their position is within a law firm, in the internet marketing space, it's easy for someone to say, "I've earned $2 million dollars just this year!" when in fact they are hoping you'll give them your $10,000 so they can pay their rent next month.

There's nothing wrong with asking for actual evidence before engaging in any professional relationship. And although mentor-mentee relationships are generally unpaid situations, you are relying on your mentor(s) to provide battle- and time-tested advice. I wouldn't want to leave my success to chance or in the hands of someone who isn't who they claim to be, and I don't advise you do that, either.

My colleague Steve Sisler, founder of The Behavioral Resource Group, says it this way:

We don't see people as they are, we see them as we are. Those who regularly fall prey to false representation within the (coaching) industry are those who tend to operate out of their limbic brain rather than their rational mind. These are emotional decision makers who "need" help as opposed to logical thinkers who want help. Regardless of where you sit on the brain wave, invite trusted friends into your decision making process. Remember the words of King Solomon; "In the multitude of counselors there is safety."

Now you have everything you need to find your perfect mentor. Once you have one, you'll never want to live without one. Next, we're going to dive into another way you can compress time and make the most of every day. If you're ready, continue reading ...

Be steady and well ordered in your life so that you can be fierce and original in your work.
—Gustave Flaubert

In order for any system or strategy to work, it's up to you to take the first step. The structure will set you free!"
—Honorée Corder (2005)

Maximize your money and your milliseconds with a mentor. You'll be so incredibly glad you did!
—Honorée Corder (2015)

Master Strategy #5:
Use Time-Multiplier Strategies

A major part of the work I have done over the past fifteen years with my coaching clients centers around the systems they have in place, don't have in place, and need and want to put in place. These systems are designed to help them increase their levels of efficiency, effectiveness, productivity, and profitability. Having solid systems in place is crucial to every aspect of life and business success, whether you're talking about the best use of time, employee recruiting and retention, business expansion, marketing, business development, or crisis management.

More than half of my clients have come to me because they're working more hours than they want to, aren't spending as much time with their families as they would like, and their hobbies are severely neglected or long since forgotten. The other half has heard my tagline: *I help professionals double their income and triple their time off.* And that's what they want. (imagine that?) It just might be what you want, too.

Multiplier Strategies

If you're like me, you want the skinny, the real information, and you want it immediately. To that end, you'll want to use **Master Strategy #5,** the intentional use of time-multiplier strategies.

Here are two of the most aggressive and effective strategies you can apply today to dramatically increase your effectiveness and efficiency immediately.

These two strategies are what I call Time Multiplier Strategies. That means they will increase and improve your current level of efficiency dramatically. A word of warning: these strategies are extremely powerful. Only use them if you're prepared for them to work!

By now you've most likely taken care of the basics of optimizing your time, such as owning a smartphone and hiring an assistant to handle your day-to-day activities. You'll get good results with the fundamentals, yet there is always a next level for you when you optimize your normal workday.

With that said, here we go!

Time Multiplier Strategy Number One: One morning hour (your power hour) equals two evening hours. Get up and into the office one or even two hours earlier than you have up until now. You will find that you can accomplish twice as much in any given early morning hour as you can in one evening hour.

Chances are you're less mentally alert in the evening, especially if you have worked a full day. That is the case for some, but not all. If your most productive hours are late at night, you can use late night hours as your power hour time. The key is to determine what time of day is your best time of day. Every person has natural rhythms, and identifying those rhythms places you in the driver's seat of your success. In coaching, I call recognizing and owning your personal rhythms as having "the edge."

My mind is most clear, focused and energized, between the hours of 7 a.m. and Noon. That is the time I dedicate to the activities that have the most impact for my businesses. Those five hours provide the equivalent of ten hours spent doing the exact same activities later in the day.

This strategy is why the world's most successful people can usually be found in their offices hours earlier than those who are less successful. To join the ranks of other outrageously successful business people, you'll want to be in your office right along with them. If you've picked up this book, you're probably not part of the pack that merely gets by, or at the very least you're tired of being among them. How do you apply this strategy? Identify the hours when you are at your best and use them to work on the key activities that grow your business.

You will use your power hour (or hours) to handle the most important aspects of your day: product development or creation, strategic planning, and implementing key systems. By doing this before anyone else even begins working, you've gained control of the flow of the rest of your day.

If you don't (or you haven't), you'll find yourself reacting to the events of the day instead of being able to respond to them. This makes you "response-able." Your power hour is when you should be focused only on actions that take you closer to your long-range goals.

This is not the time to catch up on email, schedule appointments, handle action items not requiring your full mental focus, or tackle administrative paperwork. Those tasks are time traps that use a minimum of your brainpower. If you succumb to doing them during prime work hours, you'll never gain the exponential multiplication of quality, focused time that you're after (and I know you want). Schedule these less critical items purposely because you don't need to be on your "A" game. Delegating these simple tasks to your assistant will also multiply your efficiency and effectiveness.

Here's a simple example: imagine a five-year-old boy with a small chunk of Kryptonite sneaking up on Superman while he sleeps. If Superman doesn't see him coming, he's trapped. It doesn't matter that Superman is a superior adversary. A little boy has gained control of Superman's time; consequently he is now in control of Superman.

It's the same thing with your average workday. If you start your workday when everyone else does, doing what everyone else is doing, you'll be trying to perform and produce in the most difficult of circumstances. You can't out-perform and out-produce your competition if you're doing exactly what they are doing, and at exactly the same time. Use your edge to get the edge.

Even the most efficient businessperson will lose the upper hand to the "busy-ness" of the average workday. If you try to optimize the hours between 8 a.m. and 5 p.m. beyond a certain point without being incredibly purposeful, you will fight a daily battle, trying to succeed while dealing with interruptions, urgencies, and employee challenges. You already know how these can wreak havoc on your time.

Once you begin to use your early morning power hour for long-term goal activities, you will become addicted to the powerful feeling and results only a day well spent can give you. Make this practice a habit, and your enemy (busy-ness) can never again take them away from you.

Let's take purposeful planning up a notch with ...

Time Multiplier Strategy Number Two: One weekly planning hour can yield more than 200 percent increased ability and success.

I advise my clients to spend at least one hour on Friday afternoon or over the weekend to create their Weekly Plan. This strategy allows you to block time for the people, things, and events most important to you, way ahead of time.

Perhaps you've heard of the time management metaphor where someone has a jar and must put in large rocks, small pebbles, sand, and water. Each element represents items on your to-do list in order of importance. When you put the water in first, try putting in sand and see what happens. The water gushes right back out, making a big mess in the process. Fill it up with sand, and the pebbles and rocks don't stand a chance. A few will sit on top of the sand, but the rest will fall away.

These four elements provide a metaphor for your real life. We all have the same amount of time, and yet when we do the most important action items first, represented by the rocks, we can still find time to do the other, less important, activities. But somehow, the reverse just isn't true.

The most effective way to put all four elements in is in this order: rocks (again, the most important things in your life and business), pebbles (the next most important items), sand (items with no urgency at all), and water (least important stuff to do; delegate or discard). Amazingly, these four elements will all fit into your "time jar" when you start by placing the most important items in first. If some of the smaller elements don't fit or go by the wayside, they clearly don't matter as much.

How does this translate to your life and business? By scheduling the most important things you want to accomplish in advance, you will accomplish them. The items you can, and must consciously choose, are the ones most related to your long-term goals. The first step is identifying the actions, the second step is blocking time to actually execute them.

Coach's Commandment: Block the time out to execute your most important activities, and don't let anything change your focus.

Anything, you say? Yes, anything!

I've given this intentional use of blocked time a name: "brain surgery time." Brain surgery time is a block of time on your calendar that is nonnegotiable.

Here's an analogy: five minutes from now you fall to the floor, unconscious. After being rushed to the emergency room, doctors run tests and determine you need brain surgery.

Good news! The most respected and highly skilled brain surgeon in the world is available to work on you (and miraculously, he's at the local hospital *and* covered by your insurance). He's available tomorrow from 10 a.m. until 3 p.m. to complete the five-hour surgery necessary to save your life. Can you think of any reason you would miss the opportunity to have him operate on you? Would you, perhaps, decide instead to update your Facebook status, turn in an overdue expense report, or chat on the phone with a friend about what you're going to wear to a party on Saturday night?

Of course not!

You would show up at the appointed time, ready and willing. That's how you've got to handle your schedule from now on if (and only if) you want the extraordinary results possible from doing so: show up, at the appointed time ready and willing to do whatever you've decided is important for you to do based upon your goals and outcomes.

When you schedule time to do what needs to be done, such as work on your business, spend quality time with your family, your kids, and yourself, you must treat it as brain surgery time.

You can use your schedule in much the same way: place nonnegotiable blocked time on your calendar for the purpose of achieving your goals and outcomes. Using this strategy will render you almost super human in your capacity to accomplish the seemingly impossible. Those around you will scratch their heads in wonder at your ability to produce the quality and quantity of work previously thought impossible. And you, sparky, are doing it all before noon. (You're welcome.)

Don't misunderstand me. Of course you can be flexible. I know as well as anyone that *life happens*, and when it does all you can do is ride the wave. It is during these times that you can increase your flexibility, and once the ride is over, you can once again focus on what is truly important. When life throws a curve ball, we must shift our priorities. For example, if a family member gets sick, caring for that person becomes priority number one. Taking advantage of this system when life is running smoothly allows you the flexibility to adjust when it's needed and return to your normal priorities when the crisis has passed. I've spent what seems an unnatural amount of time juggling and moving pre-scheduled blocks of time, and you probably will as well.

Staying connected with your desired outcomes and putting time on your calendar to accomplish them will help you do just that: accomplish them. And guess what? You'll be so proud of yourself when you accomplish them, *and* this will build your accomplishment muscles ... which will lead you to becoming more inspired to do more of what you want to do ... which will lead to—well, I don't know exactly what it will lead to, but I promise you you're gonna love it!

We all have the same 24 hours each day.
The difference between your future success or
failure is up to you, your attitude, and where
you focus your time.
—Honorée Corder

Brain Surgery Time in Action

Turn off your phone(s), your internet access (and the television, if you work at home like I do), and put yourself in a room alone. The time has come to block out what's most important to you.

Right now, schedule an hour each week to do your planning as a recurring appointment on your calendar. My weekly recurrent appointment is from 3–4 p.m. on Friday afternoons.

First, I review my goals and my progress on them during the previous week. Second, I ask myself the same questions I suggest you ask yourself:

- *What is the most important action item I can take toward achieving my goals next week?*
- *When can I block out time to get those items accomplished?*

Make a list of these items. Estimate the amount of time you'll need to get them done. I don't usually work in blocks longer than two to three hours, unless I absolutely have to, which often requires multiday appointments. You might need to do that, too.

In addition, ask yourself these questions:

- *Who needs to hear from me (clients/customers, vendors, potential business, prospects, business partners, investors)?* Remember to reference your 100-Day Plan for reminders.
- *Who needs to see me (family, friends, and perhaps you need a little time for yourself)?*
- *What needs to be done, organized, planned, and executed?*

Make time for each action item you've identified on your calendar, and yes, some items will spill over to coming weeks. That's okay, planning your schedule in advance will only serve you in the long run. Best-case scenario, you finish ahead of schedule and find yourself with blocks of time you can use for other important projects. A reasonable scenario is to use each time block for completing the project on time. The worst-case scenario is you use every minute of blocked time and end up needing more. I know from experience that you will eventually be able to estimate how much time each project will need within an hour or two (at the most). The added bonus is you will eliminate any propensity you have toward procrastination because you will feel great as you accomplish the things you set out to do.

Using these two time-multiplier strategies will produce a huge difference right away. Your productivity will skyrocket to more than double or even triple what it has been in the past. Another added benefit is you will also be energized by all you've accomplished, including any personal or nonbusiness related items. No longer will you have a to-do list with items you never seem to finish. There is nothing as fantastic as crossing items off of your to-do list, completing projects, and knowing you are consistently producing at your highest level.

Pay any price to stay in the presence of extraordinary people.
—Mike Murdock

The only difference between where you are this year and where you are next, are the books you read, the people you meet, and the actions you take.
—Charlie "Tremendous" Jones

You will eventually rise to the level of the people you hang around with—whether you hang around millionaires or idiots.
—Honorée Corder (2005)

Will you be successful because you do extraordinary work or have extraordinary relationships? YES.
—Honorée Corder (2015)

TALL ORDER!

Master Strategy #6:
The Power of Association

Who and what you have in your life determines whether or not you succeed. Harsh? Perhaps. True? Absolutely. You see, your environment, which is comprised of your home, where you work, your friends, and your associates, determines with great accuracy whether you will be successful ... or not.

Master Strategy #6 consists of harnessing the power of association. Whom you associate with, and whom you have in your intimate and inner circles, can make or break you.

More than a decade ago, when I was building my network marketing business in earnest, I easily found lots of people who wanted my lifestyle. What they didn't always want was to do the work it took to achieve it! For less than $200 you can start your own business. Almost with the snap of your fingers, bam! You're in business. What most people don't realize is the hard work, focus, and determination it takes to yield an income of six- and seven-figure levels.

Of course I heard a lot of "sign me up for that!" meaning, of course, my income and lifestyle ... not necessarily the hard work that needed for it to actually happen.

I remember finding it frustrating to want to coach, mentor, and develop my business partners to a respectable income level, only to have some of them quit after a short time (and usually moments inches before they were about to see the big results they desired). The residual income I still enjoy today, a dozen years after I stopped focusing on building that business, is a result of the effort I put in all of those years ago. I'm saddened to think of all of the people I couldn't convince that continuing their efforts would pay off long after they stopped focusing on their business if they would just keep going until they hit their tipping point.

The First Question

A very dear friend and respected colleague of mine called at the peak of my displeasure, and I still remember that destiny-changing phone call. He asked me a particularly powerful question, one of the best I have ever heard: "Do you realize that success in business (or life) is determined not in who you hire, but in who you fail to fire?" His question hit me like a ton of bricks. It wasn't necessarily that I was only hiring the wrong people, it was also very possible I wasn't eliminating them quickly enough from my life or my business.

His question prompted me to revisit my vision of the ultimate business partner and also to ask some other important questions.

- What are the qualities and characteristics of the people I really want to work with?
- What would I expect of them, and of myself, in our ongoing relationship?
- How would I determine if they are the right fit not just for right now, but also for the foreseeable future?

These questions helped me to begin to pick people to work with who were equally as committed as I was to their success. I stated my expectations of them and told them what they could expect from me. I asked them to tell me why working with me was important not only for the short term, but over the long term. This affected my business then, much the same way it affects my businesses today, in two ways: First, I'm better at identifying the signs and determining whom I might want to be in a long-term relationship (business or personal) with. Second, I'm as clear as I can be in my expectations. Therefore my relationships tend to be better and are getting better all the time.

Not long after I starting asking these powerful questions of myself, I was contemplating a huge career change. Having just accomplished my long-term business goals, I was quickly losing interest in my career. I'll be honest, life was great! I had attended my company's international convention and received multiple awards. My income was substantial and sustaining. Yet internally, I was unsettled and knew it was time to move to another level.

Then, Another Question

Just as I started to listen to my inner voice and think about what type of change I might need to make, another powerful phone call changed the trajectory of my life. A longtime friend asked me the mother of all power questions, the answer to which still impacts my life even today:

"Who do you have in your life asking you a better question every single day, challenging you to be the best you can be?"

I had relayed to her how unsettled I felt, and she knew me well enough to know it would be easy for me to stay in my comfort zone, ignore my restlessness, and become complacent.

In truth, while I had lots of loving and wonderful people around me, the number of people challenging me to be my best on a daily basis was almost zero. I realized that in order to take my life to the next level, I needed a level of support that did not exist for me. I needed to find more people living the life I aspired to live, who would be willing to push me, pull me, entice me, and encourage me each and every day. With her encouragement and that of my coach and a few close friends, I made the decision to change careers.

Looking back, I had no idea I would become a sought-after speaker, trainer, business and executive coach, and as of this writing, a 17-time author. That one question, and the decision to make a change, altered my destiny. Once I stepped through the fear and made the decision to transition, everything fell into place. It still is, all of these years later, and I am so incredibly grateful for my life today.

These two questions, at exactly the right times in my life, gave me ultimate clarity. They revealed to me that the choices I was making in my relationships and business were holding me back and not allowing me to move forward.

How does this relate to you? Perhaps the people around you don't bring out the best in you. They don't challenge you to expect results you think may be impossible. Maybe your career isn't the best fit. Are you living in an environment that you don't absolutely love?

You can't know what effect you will set in motion by embracing change and building a future that is entirely different than the course you are on today. Having the nerve to listen to your intuition, to fearlessly answer tough questions, and hear the revelatory answers that come with them is not for the weak.

It would be much easier for you to retreat into the safety of the life you know now, stay the course, and stick with who and what you've always known. No one would blame you if you stayed put and kept going on your current path. In fact, there would be plenty of people who would breathe a sign of relief if you kept the status quo. Becoming all you can be serves as an example for those around you, and some people don't want to be around a shining example of what they don't have the courage to do themselves.

But you won't know how great your life can be unless and until you do a hard swallow and jump. Please jump. I strongly encourage you to jump!

Coach's Observation: Here's what happens when you take control of your environment, including everyone and everything in it:

- You'll suddenly have tons more energy! Things will happen faster, more easily, and with better results than ever before.
- You will be much more creative!
- You'll create synergy with the old and new people in your life, which will automatically take you higher.
- You'll have much less stress! As you streamline the details of your life, you will shed old baggage and create more room for new and exciting opportunities.

What are you tolerating?

In coaching, I talk a lot to my clients about "tolerations." Tolerations are those things that zap your energy, annoy you, and drain away your effectiveness, happiness, and success. They make you less attractive to yourself, and therefore, less attractive to others. Tolerations can be people, activities, or even some of the places you go.

The people in your life are crucial to your success, but they can also contribute to your failure. Think about each person in your life: are they supportive of your vision? Your goals? Do they ask you empowering and, if necessary, tough questions? Or do they predict failure, doom, or worse? Be aware of what your friends, family, and associates bring to your life.

What about your work, or where you work? When you wake up in the morning, are you excited to begin working because your work environment jazzes you? Do you look forward to seeing or working with the people you are currently working with, or when you see their names or faces do you internally cringe with dread? Is your office or work space comfortable or even inspiring? Notice how you feel about what, when, where, and with whom you get to work.

Is your home your sanctuary? Did you know it even could be? Do you feel comfortable, relaxed, creative, and alive there? Or is it a cluttered, disorganized environment that causes you daily stress?

With every toleration, you have three options:

1. **Change them.** You can change the "who, what, where, when, or why," until you get your desired results.
2. **Eliminate them.** If something or someone doesn't serve you, perhaps it is time for them to go! You won't need to usher people out of your life, just keep your distance. Look at it this way: there are many people you want to stay in touch with, people you admire ... But those relationships that are no longer in your best interest can be allowed to fade away. It's that easy. Dealing with objects is easier; you can give them away, donate them, or simply throw them away.
3. **Accept them.** You can't always donate or give away your spouse, mother, or

sister. You might have founded a company, and it turns out your investors are going to be around for a bit longer. Sometimes our own personal sanity requires us to accept things as they are, rather than making ourselves crazy trying to control or change the situation. Sometimes circumstances are what they are. Let it go, if that is truly the only choice you have right now.

By taking control of your immediate environment, you reclaim your personal power and create a healthy, focused foundation for your future. Your life and how happy you are in it is entirely up to you. Make everything about your relationships, your career, and your life the exact way you want them to be.

*Surround yourself with people who are
going to lift you higher.*
—Oprah Winfrey

*Don't change to be like others.
Be yourself and the right people will love you.*
—Unknown

*Stop trying to fit in
because you were born to stand out!*
—Unknown

*Be purposeful as you choose
your inner circle, for your ten
closest friends determine your destiny.*
—Honorée Corder

Master Strategy #7:
Unlock Your Super Alter Ego with a Coach

Winners in nearly every profession know that without the right coaches, they won't perform at their peak, and with the right coaches, the sky is the limit. World-class athletes know it. So do CEOs of major corporations.

Now a select number of business people know it, too: as the economy putters along, organizations flatten or outsource their production overseas, production cycles hit hyper-speed, and as change becomes a constant, coaches can help you become a better, more nimble, effective, and efficient business leader.

Master Strategy #7 is the use of a coach! I absolutely believe everyone needs a coach. Not because I have spent the better part of fifteen years as a coach, but because I have a full complement of coaches!

Flash back to my network marketing days: I had achieved a top-level position and was doing everything I needed to do to reach my goals and objectives within the fastest possible timeframe. Or at least that's what I thought.

The CEO of my company called to offer me a business coach and my first thoughts were, *What could I possibly need with a coach?! I'm already doing great!* Fortunately, I kept my mouth shut, accepted the incredible gift of a coach, and I'm so glad I did. Within 90 days, I had increased my overall productivity and income by 300 percent. The insights I made about myself, the way I was using my time, identifying bigger goals, defining a larger vision, and being held accountable were all crucial to me.

My coach did what coaches do: she saw what I wasn't able to see. She helped me take risks, eliminate obstacles, and fully step into my potential. I still use the services of at least one coach on an ongoing basis, and right now I have several coaches each with their own area of specialty.

When I meet someone who doesn't have a coach, they usually have the same excuse: *I can't afford a coach.* I simply shake my head: if you think you can't afford a coach, that's exactly why you need one! I often wish there was something I could say to change their mind. If this is one of your objections, perhaps this chapter can help you see the light.

What Does a Coach Do?

A coach's function is multifaceted: to blend insights, tools, and key traits to move their clients toward success in many areas, both on the job and off. Performers at all levels are elevated to greater advancement in the presence of an effective coach. No matter what, a coach serves as a sounding board and strategist. A great coach will help you make sense of challenging situations, and encourage you to adopt systems and plans to help you get where you want to go faster, more easily, and with much less effort, all while putting more and more money in your pocket almost immediately and over the long term.

The value of coaching is clearly understood in the world of sports. Tiger Woods needs a myriad of coaches to excel. If the number one golfer in the world relies on the power of coaching, wouldn't anyone in the business world benefit from applying the same practice?

I would venture to guess that not a day goes by when Tiger Woods doesn't speak with his head coach or work with his form coach to fine-tune his chip shot, drive, or putt. Yet many people step into business and leadership positions with little direction and few goals or strategies for growth and development. Rarely do they seek help acquiring leadership skills or identifying hidden strengths, instead they try to figure it out on their own.

Self-study will get you only so far. To truly move into the fast lane on the super highway of success, you'll need at least one coach holding you accountable and helping you make key decisions.

Who is a Coach for?

Choosing to have a great coach in your corner can accelerate your success beyond anything you can comprehend. Having an incredible coach is like signing up for TSA Prev√ at the airport. Go ahead and stand in line, you might risk missing your flight. Go through the Prev√-check line, and you'll be at your gate in no time. If you're the kind of person who would opt for the Prev√, then a coach is definitely the right choice for you.

Coaches are not for the meek or for people who want someone to cosign their BS. Coaches are for people who value direct and unambiguous feedback. The best coaches have one thing in common: they are mercilessly results-oriented. They will tell you the truth, even if that truth includes a gut-check moment. They want for you the very best of everything, and they want to see you get it in the least amount of time, with the least amount of investment.

I have and have had several incredible coaches. While at first I hesitated to share my true aspirations as well as my deepest fears and doubts, I quickly learned that having a solid and brilliant coach was my ticket to everything I desired. Now I have several coaches who hold my hand, walk with me through challenges, inspire me to be my best, and yes, give me straight and sometimes unwanted feedback. While incredibly uncomfortable, I am always grateful on the other side because of the massive benefits I see as a result. I drink from the wells of my coaches' knowledge like having a tall glass of iced tea on a hot Texas day. I can't wait to see what will come of our conversations, and I know when you find the right coach for you, you will feel something similar.

Coaching is truly product development, and you are the product. You get to choose which piece or part of your life or business needs your focus and hire a coach for just that area. There are business coaches, executive coaches, speech or presentation coaches, image coaches, life coaches, health coaches, relationship coaches … the list goes on and on.

Chosen carefully, a competent coach is worth their weight in gold, and the return on your investment in a coach can be many, many times any amount of time or money. A great coach will feel like a solid investment because they charge what they are worth. I know I'm always happy to pay the fees—I actually look forward to it, because I know what I will get in return, and I can't wait to get it!

Coaching versus Therapy

I'm asked quite often what is the difference between coaching and therapy. The best way I can describe the difference is this: Therapy is a process to help one deal with their past and the challenges and wounds that are the result of incidents and happenings in that past. Said another way, therapy aids you in addressing your past, which is every day you've lived up until today.

Conversely, coaching is specifically for the purpose of helping you design the future you want to create and to create that future in the shortest amount of time humanly possible.

I've suggested a therapeutic environment for many of my clients, and I've benefitted from several therapists myself. There is a time and place for both skill sets; the use of either or both at different times on your journey can be amazing.

Coaching is the means through which we come to realize our greatest potential.
—Ryan C. Browning (one of my coaches)

How to Get the Most out of Your Coach

Making the most of your coaching experience will bring you more joy than you can fathom. Because I want you to use coaching and love it as much as I do, and because I speak from both the coach and client perspective, here are some tips and insights you might want to implement while on your coaching journey:

Your coach should share their policies and procedures with you at the start. Here are a couple of mine:

All conversations and their contents are completely confidential. Regardless of who is paying the bill, I will not discuss the contents of a coaching session with any third party unless I have advance permission. If your coach doesn't mention it, I advise you to insist on complete confidentiality between the coach and yourself. That means all conversations are private and sacred at the time they occur and forever after. Actually, confidentiality should be part of the coaching agreement you sign. But if your boss or company is generous enough to provide coaching, you may never see the agreement, so ask your coach what their policy is.

I never acknowledge someone is a client in public. Coaching is not unlike therapy in that you may not want anyone to know just how you got to a place of being so full of awesomeness and excellence. Your coach should not acknowledge you are a client to anyone else unless you give permission. What you are doing, how you are doing, what you have accomplished, and your personal secrets are not discussed or even hinted at with anyone else. People may know you are working with a coach, and may ask how you are doing. Your coach's standard answer should be "He/she is doing just fine." (Period.)

Many of my clients can't gush enough to others about our coaching relationship, and all I do is nod and smile. A great coach will stay quiet even when they don't have to.

Insist on setting measurable outcomes for the duration of your initial coaching period, and objectives for each conversation. To ensure that your work with a coach doesn't become a series of unproductive conversations, tie everything to a business or personal benefit. By itself, "improve time-management skills" has no measurable benefit, and frankly, is immeasurable. However, it is a legitimate way to achieve a critical goal: "meet project deadlines in 30 percent less time." Work with your coach to ensure your targets are measureable and well defined.

Set measurable and tangible goals. Coaching provides an opportunity to create an environment for achieving stretch goals. Aim for improvements that you know you can achieve with the right plan, intention, and actions. Most people aren't using even half of their cylinders, so don't be surprised if working with a coach feels like kicking your achievements into overdrive. I suggest you not strive for maximum improvement in any coaching period, keep it simple and achievable in bite-sized pieces. A 15 percent improvement would be an incredible start and is the difference between a mediocre player and a star.

When it comes to assessing your performance, ask your coach to be exhaustively honest with you. Some are not.

Take these sound bites of coaches describing their role: "I'm just there to hold the CEO's hand," said one. "I'm like a trusted family friend," said another. Or, "My job is to remind him, 'your greatest strength is that you're you.'" Ummm, *no.*

If you get a warm and fuzzy feeling from a business coach (or any coach for that matter), run! Look for a coach who isn't afraid to use straightforward, constructive criticism. Coaches are at their best when they insist on helping you to get to your best, when they push you out of your comfort zone and don't let you back in.

I know I've withheld feedback because I can sometimes sense my clients might take my assessments too personally. If at any point you aren't getting what you want, or you sense your coach is keeping a little in reserve, ask for exactly what you want. If you ask me, I'm going to tell you. But I'm always going to do it thoughtfully and with heart.

Your coach's agenda should be your agenda. I begin each session with a carefully thought-out purpose for that session. But I almost always ask, *What would you like to discuss, or what outcome would you like to obtain, during this session?* In other words, I always arrive at a session with an agenda based upon previous conversations, and the Coach Call Maximizer (pre-session homework) I received in advance of our session. Many times, however, my clients show up without having turned in their homework (ahem) or with breaking news that needs to be discussed. I let my clients drive the bus, but my motor is running, too, just in case. A coach should be holding your previously stated outcomes, visions, and goals up for you at each session and helping you to stay the course.

Take ownership of your coaching and client-coach relationship. You absolutely must ask for what you want and need. Your responsibility is to make sure you show up, on time and ready, for each session. Trust me when I say you'll want to force yourself to prepare for each session until you get addicted to the results you can get only from coaching. Then you'll do it without my (or your coach's) prompting.

Are You Ready for Coaching?

If you're ready to consider hiring a coach, you are deciding to embark on a magnificent journey! Coaching is proven to work when two factors are present:

1. The client is willing to grow.
2. There is a gap (or several gaps) between where they are now and where they want to be.

The presence of these two elements are all that is necessary for you and your coach to address and resolve challenges, create new focus and direction, get in the best physical and mental shape of your life, move your business in the right direction, dramatically increase sales and profitability, or devise and execute a plan of action.

As you interview and look to hire a coach, you will most likely enroll in specific programs that can include focus on any of the following:

Coaching for skills. The focus is on a specific task or skill set. You may want to get better at making presentations, preparing a solid business plan to get quality investors, or even writing your first book.

Coaching for performance. Here, the focus is on improving existing job performance. For example, you might focus on developing systems to accurately evaluate employee performance.

Coaching for development. This type of coaching involves a concentration on an individual's future career path. A terrific career coach can help you do everything from developing your resume, to swiftly and successfully navigating the interview process, choosing the next best landing spot, and making tactical and strategic choices every step of the way.

Coaching on a variety of topics. This program recognizes that executives can be lonely and frequently need insight, perspective, and constructive feedback on both personal and business issues. It could also include developing specific leadership skills such as emotional intelligence.

With some great coaching, you will compress the amount of time it takes to reach your goals. You will also have someone who believes in you, holds your vision for you, and can keep you moving in just the right direction. I know you will benefit and enjoy having a coach as much as I do!

"A Coach is someone who tells you what you don't want to hear, who has you see what you don't want to see, so you can be who you have always known you could be.
—Tom Landry

Ability is what you're capable of doing. Motivation determines what you do. Attitude determines how well you do it.
—Coach Lou Holtz

Coaching is a series of conversations, encouragements, and ideas that lead to the creation of your destiny.
—Honorée Corder (2005)

With the right coach, your vision isn't a maybe, it's your eventuality.
—Honorée Corder (2015)

Rocket Fuel

Congratulations! You've completed this book, which to me is a sure sign of your excellence as well as your upcoming magnificent success. Clearly you are internally motivated, and the internally motivated people in this world are the most successful overall.

In this book, I have given you some of my most used, tried and true tips, tools, strategies and ideas. I know they work, each and every one of them, because I have used them in the past for great results. I consistently return to them over and over again because I want to create greater future success. They are the same ones I discuss with my clients and audience members on a regular basis.

A Few Parting Words

On anyone's journey to success, there are dozens of tiny steps that get you to the top of the mountain. It is easy, in our world today, to want instant gratification. I know, I have wanted it all now for about twenty-five years. I hear you! While this book is short and sweet, and by its virtue makes it seem like the path to achievement is short and sweet, I know from experience it is anything but ...

I say, "Sad but true, there are no shortcuts." Yet one of the most amazing things I've learned on my journey is that the journey is interesting. Every single project, book, presentation, or even business-at-large has taken longer than I would have liked to complete, been more frustrating at times than I would have preferred, and cost more in blood, sweat, tears, and loss of sleep than anyone could have forecasted. HOWEVER, the journey has 150,000 percent been worth it. If at any point I had taken a different or easier path, I wouldn't be sitting here, writing these words of encouragement and inspiration for you to read.

If I were in front of you right now, I would implore you to, no matter what, *keep going*. In the face of delays, denials, and discombobulations, do yourself a favor and focus and refocus and refocus and refocus (as many times as you need to) on reaching your goals and living your vision. You will miss out on lots of amazing stuff if you don't.

The world will miss out if you do not become all you were put on this Earth to become.

I don't want you to miss out, I don't want the world to miss out, and I don't want to miss out. I'm sitting here, cheering you on, waiting for you to grab the brass ring, squeal with excitement as your cross the finish line, and jump up and down when you win.

So Here's What You Gotta Do Now (Right now!)

Follow the steps exactly as I've outlined them. Each idea in this book is design built and intended to be stacked one on top of the other as a framework for you to use. They will help you to clear away obstacles, which will move you more easily toward your goals and enable you to obtain your vision.

If you've already created your vision, I know you feel you're on fire, invincible even, and are raring to go. If you haven't, and you might not have because you wanted to read the whole book first, I understand. Schedule a time to create your vision as soon as possible. Then, read your vision twice a day, like clockwork. It will re-motivate you every time you lay eyes on it, and you'll need that motivation (some days more than others) to keep going.

Have you created a plan based upon your vision? If yes, great. If not, put that on the schedule, too. A solid plan will cement the feeling in your heart that anything is possible for you (it is) and keep you moving in the direction your soul desires.

Your plan will contain some inspiring and perhaps intimidating goals. You can get them! Those goals you've identified, once achieved, set the stage for even bigger goals later.

Do you have a tribe? People who inspire you to be a better person, hold you accountable, and give you insights and much-needed information? If you do, good on you! Consider yourself one lucky person. If not, go on a mission to find (and keep) those people who desire for you what you desire for yourself, and will help you get there. The people you need on your team will be a mentor and a coach (or seven). Start looking for them right away.

On a continual basis, ask yourself great questions, keep the faith, and remember: you've got this!

I have created an amazing life using what I've shared with you in this book, and I know you can, too. My best wishes for your greatest future success!

If opportunity doesn't knock,
build a door.
—Milton Berle

Climb high; Climb far.
Your goal the sky; your aim the star.
—Inscription at Williams College

You've got what it takes, and it will take
everything you've got.
—Unknown

Go get 'em, tiger!
—Honorée Corder

Get Even More

AS A THANK YOU FOR reading this book, I want to give you two free chapters of:

Business Dating: Applying Relationship Rules in Business for Ultimate Success

This is my networking book that shows you exactly how the rules of personal dating apply to your professional relationships. Go here and tell me where to send your free chapters:

http://honoreecorder.com/businessdating

<u>Gratitude</u>

To Byron—I couldn't do any of this without your love and support. Thank you and I love you!

To Lexi—I'm blessed and grateful to be your mom every single day.

To my assistant Christina, whose brilliance sparkles every day! I am so grateful for you!

To the incredible individuals who made writing and publishing this book possible: the clients I've worked with for the past 15 years, the successful professionals who allowed me to share their stories; my editing team Alyssa and Leslie; and Dino for designing this and all of my gorgeous book covers ... thank you, thank you!

Who Is Honorée

Honorée Corder is the best-selling author of a many books, including:

- *Prosperity for Writers: A Writer's Guide to Creating Abundance*
- *Prosperity for Writers Productivity Journal: A Writer's Workbook for Creating Abundance;*
- *Business Dating: Applying Relationship Rules in Business for Ultimate Success;*
- *If Divorce is a Game, These are the Rules;*
- *Vision to Reality: How Short Term Massive Action Equals Long Term Results;*
- *The Successful Single Mom* book series;
- *The Successful Single Dad;*
- *Play2Pay;*
- *Paying4College: How to Save 25-50% on Your Child's College Education;*
- and the original *Tall Order! 7 Master Strategies to Organize Your Life and Double Your Success in Half the Time.*

She is also a serial entrepreneur, keynote speaker, and executive coach. She empowers others to dream big, clarify their vision, and turn that vision into reality.

Find out more at HonoreeCorder.com

Honorée Enterprises, LLC
Honoree@HonoreeCorder.com
http://www.HonoreeCorder.com
Twitter: @Honoree @Singlemombooks
Facebook: http://www.facebook.com/Honoree
Instagram: @Honoree